Praise for *Smart*

"Frank uses his own story and mistakes to help make essential money concepts relatable and understandable. He shares what he learned through his own mistakes and the actions he took to take his business from "struggling" to extremely successful. I think this is what makes Frank's book so extremely helpful. Frank is real, relatable, and he makes the complex and intimidating topic of money much easier to grasp. I guarantee the information in this book and the way it is presented will help you take your business to the next level!"

– Amanda Mittleman MS, Owner, **Mo-Mentum Fitness**,
Huntington Beach CA
Todd Durkin Mastermind Fit Pro of The Year, 2016
IDEA World Fitness Personal Trainer of The Year Nominee, 2016

"After reading Coach Pucher's book, I can see all the valuable information needed when starting as a solo entrepreneur. I wish I had access to him 9 years ago when I first opened. His nuggets will allow someone to not only see their dream on paper but make it a reality. You do not see all the small details when you first decide to spread your wings and open a business, but with Frank's advice, you can slowly grow your job into a PROFITABLE BUSINESS."

– Matthew Stocker, Owner, Trinity Fitness, Easton, PA

"I know Frank through a Mastermind and Mentorship program both my wife and I are involved in. I have the unique perspective of being a 25-year Financial Industry professional, and my spouse has been in the fitness industry for over 25 years. This is a very heartfelt, focused, personal, and vulnerable expression of looking beyond your work place and looking in the mirror to honestly assess whether or not you are doing what you should be doing for yourself and your family! It's not just about making more money. It's about having a plan and planning wisely. Having no plan is a plan to fail! In this book Frank makes you believe in yourself, takes you outside your comfort zone and acts as a role model for Fiscal Fitness. Learn from experience and help yourself be whatever 'successful' means to you!"

– Robert Davis,
Sr. Vice President and Institutional Consultant, Winter Park, FL

Smart Money Moves

A Practical Approach
to Earning, Growing and
Protecting Your Money

by **Frank Pucher**

TABLE OF CONTENTS

I

THE FIRST RULE OF MONEY:
DON'T LOSE MONEY

II

THE SECOND RULE OF MONEY:
MAKE MORE MONEY

III

THE THIRD RULE OF MONEY:
PROTECT AND GROW YOUR WEALTH

IV

DEVELOP YOUR GAME PLAN

To my fellow fitness professionals,
this book is dedicated to you.

For those of you who wake up early, sipping coffee in
your car on your way to the early morning sessions,
to those who work late serving the needs of your
clients. Thank you. The work you do is important,
and you deserve more than you receive.

The lessons in this book are my gift to you.

ACKNOWLEDGEMENTS

Francesca – We have learned these lessons together, and this book would not be possible without our shared sacrifices.

My Team at Fitness 121 – For making each day at work not feel like work. We laugh, we share, we make a difference in the lives of others.

Larry – For believing. Your words have always inspired me, but the actions you have taken have truly spoken more than any words ever could. We are moving on from the dirt roads of yesterday, and I'm grateful for the opportunity to pave this path with you.

Todd – It wasn't a coincidence that we connected when we did. I was in search of something and the opportunity to join your MASTERMIND was the beginning of my growth, both personally and professionally. I am proud to call you a mentor and a friend.

Jenn (Mama Bear) – For being a great teammate and colleague. Thank you for your honesty and your strength. You are a great coach, and I'm proud of you!

Jarod – Thank you for allowing me to share my truth without hesitation or reservation. I appreciate the gift of your friendship.

Adina – For your friendship and your integrity. You make everyone around you better. I'm grateful for you.

Kelli – This book wouldn't be possible without your subtle nudge and helpfulness during the editing process. Thank you for all you do for so many. Yin/Yang still make the best team!

Rick – When the student was ready, you appeared. I'll pass along the importance of the fundamentals so that others, too, can GROW.

Anthony (Tony) – For teaching me the importance of knowing my numbers and not just the bottom line.

To everyone at Scriptor Publishing and those who contributed testimonials toward the book.

ABOUT THE AUTHOR

Frank Pucher is a coach, presenter and award-winning fitness entrepreneur. He opened Fitness 121 Personal Training in 1998 and currently runs his business in Roseland, NJ. Fitness 121 was twice named "NJ's Best Fitness Studio" (NJ Monthly Magazine) and has been New Jersey's "Best Personal Training Studio" (Suburban Essex Magazine of NJ) for the past four years. They continue to specialize in one-on one training and currently generate over one million dollars in annual revenue.

Frank is also a Platinum Level Coach in the Todd Durkin Mastermind Program and works with fitness professionals all over the world. Through enhanced coaching and accountability, he improves their lives, both personally and professionally.

Frank is an industry speaker and presenter and was a finalist for IDEA's Personal Trainer of the Year Award. He has completed several IRONMAN triathlons and especially enjoys good food, great wines and warm weather destinations.

FOREWORD

In the summer of my freshman year of high school, I walked into my first gym to start training for the upcoming football season. I thought I was a pretty tough kid even before I felt the true feeling of taking my body and mind to its very edge. However, when I walked into that magical place and smelled the iron, I was admittedly nervous, scared and intimidated. My palms were even sweaty, but within moments as I heard the sounds of dumbbells clanking, music cranking, people grunting, groaning and laughing, I became inspired and motivated to challenge myself.

Those emotions have not lessened in the 25+ years since. Not even a speck. In fact, I'm more passionate about fitness, training, performance and helping others be their very best physically, mentally and emotionally than I have ever been. To me, the gym isn't just a place where you work on your body to get stronger, faster, or perform better, it's a place that connects you with friends for life and gives you the confidence and inner strength to dominate anything that comes your way. It's the place that fills you up with positive emotions, lights up the darkness and reminds you that you are not alone.

After spending a majority of my life in the business of fitness, I know that many other fitness professionals share the same feelings. The 'best of the best' are truly passionate about transforming, enhancing and enriching the lives of others. It's in their blood, and they sleep, eat and breathe training. They invest thousands of hard-earned dollars in their training and education to ensure that their programs are safe and effective – even if they can barely afford it.

Let me say that again, "even if they can barely afford it."

You see, most of us didn't get into this business with the thought of driving luxury cars and living in big houses. We did it because we couldn't imagine doing anything else. It's our purpose in life.

Working in a cubicle or an office environment? NO WAY.

We wake up at 4 a.m., or even earlier, to serve others, and we do it with a smile. We train ourselves with every little pocket of time. We eat out of Tupperware containers throughout the day and drink oceans of water to stay hydrated. It's quite the life!

But is it?

Wouldn't life as a Fit Pro be much more fulfilling if we were paid our true worth for our passion and be able to afford a desirable lifestyle outside of the gym? I firmly believe so, and that's why this book is going to be the game changer – heck, life changer – for your business and your career. It's also written by one of the most authentic and experienced fitness veterans on the planet.

Frank Pucher, a.k.a. "The Doctor" as we like to affectionately call him, is as passionate about the business of fitness as they come, and I'm lucky enough to learn from him and call him a brother. Frank spends the majority of his time not just working IN his business, but ON it. He coaches fitness professionals world-wide, shares his own hard lessons learned, as well as the best practices of those he works with. He's very giving of his time and knowledge. And unlike, most fitness entrepreneurs, he's not afraid to talk about money and take action on his own business to live the awesome life he now lives (I think he's actually down in sunny Miami escaping the Jersey winter weather with his beautiful wife, Francesca, as I write this!).

What we all have to realize is that we ARE business owners. We must expand our knowledge beyond fitness and educate ourselves on how to maximize our business acumen and manage our money effectively. It saddens me when I witness a passionate fitness professional leave the industry for a career in something much less satisfying and enlightening because they need more money to support themselves and their family. That's called a job and simply working for a paycheck stinks no matter how many dollar signs are on that piece of paper.

Get paid for your passion.

A quick piece of advice before you dig deep into "Smart Money Moves," make sure you have a fresh, new highlighter. Maybe consider two because this is a book of business nuggets that you will want to keep near at all times. Building your business never stops. Sales is not a bad word and marketing happens every day. And if you manage and strive to increase your money in all aspects of your business and life with maniacal focus, Frank's collection of real life experiences and advice will become your "bible" for success.

Read this book. Do not procrastinate. Take action on Coach Frank's initiatives.

WORK like an Athlete and become a champion in business and life.

In the trenches with ya',

Jarod Cogswell

Coach, Author, Presenter and Founder of WORK like an Athlete

My hope with this book is that you will not only become more comfortable talking and thinking about money, but that you'll take ACTION on something I share within these pages.

INTRODUCTION

In 1996, I left a good paying job as a salaried personal trainer with a crazy idea to go out on my own and train people in their homes. I figured, "I'm a great personal trainer. This will be easy." And it was. I gave my boss six weeks' notice, ordered some business cards, bought a new laptop computer, and even had t-shirts made to hand out to my new clients. But after several months into my leap of faith, I found myself with just three clients, a dried-up bank account and a pile of t-shirts in my closet. Over the next few months, things went from bad to worse. I was behind on my rent, driving without auto insurance, running my car on fumes and living on a diet of water, ramen noodles and mustard. This was not the entrepreneurial dream I had envisioned.

Looking back, I was so ill-prepared to start a business because there was no capital behind me – no safety net, no established book of business upon which I could rely, no real plan. I simply had a love for what I did and a hope that that would be enough. It wasn't. There were difficult days and some lonely nights, but just when things couldn't get any worse, I was introduced (by a friend) to a new client, who thankfully paid me in cash upon our first meeting. With my car on empty, I immediately put gas in my car before going to the market, where I bought more ramen noodles and a fresh jar of mustard. A few days later, during our session, my new client asked if I had time to train his wife, "Uh, yeah!" One hour later, he was handing me another fistful of cash, and finally, over the coming weeks, with a new network of contacts, I caught some wind at my back.

By 1998, I had stabilized my finances enough to take another leap of faith, I was going to rent a

2000-square foot space and open my first brick and mortar studio. Once again, I had no real business plan other than a love for what I did.

Over the next ten years, the worst possible thing happened…we actually made some money.

You might be asking, *"How can making money be the worst possible thing?"*

The answer:

When the money you are making isn't equal to the money you're about to lose.

In 2008, I applied for and received a $300,000 SBA (Small Business Association) loan to relocate, renovate and equip my personal training studio in a spectacular building just a few miles away. This money, in addition to the $500,000 home mortgage I took out just months earlier, meant I had $800,000 worth of debt in my name when the recession hit and the economy crashed. Between a bi-weekly payroll, business rent, my new mortgage and property taxes, I knew that the numbers weren't going to add up. Something had to give.

There were weeks in a row that I needed to tell my wife (who also worked with me) that "we" couldn't take a paycheck. It was for *the good of the business,* I explained. And while she understood, I'm not sure this made her feel better about it. There were months that the business rent went unpaid. I had a difficult conversation with my landlords that despite doing my best, I was unable to make payroll and still pay the rent. They reluctantly allowed me to reduce my rent payments in agreement for a contract that back-loaded rent towards the end of my lease. I signed this out of pure desperation, as I really had no other option. My wife and I both poured our personal savings into the business to ensure that our team got paid and the SBA Loan was covered. Think about that; we weren't getting paid but instead took our savings to make sure that others did. That's not how business is supposed to work, is it? My wife and I also began discussions about losing the house, as it was now worth less than what we owed on it. My head was spinning in so many directions trying to figure out just how to get out of this mess.

Life has a way of always being darkest before the dawn. My dawn began when my MASTERMIND team helped me to see that it was my ego that was the biggest enemy. I didn't need a BIGGER facility, I needed a better one. I didn't need to invest in new equipment, I needed to invest in our culture. I finally admitted that there was much I never learned because I was running my business like a hobby and not a business like it needed to be.

Perhaps you can relate?

I share my story because many fitness professionals entertain similar thoughts. They have a belief that *SUCCESS* is somehow more likely if they take the leap of entrepreneurship.

"Leap and the net shall appear," they proclaim!

NO.

Leap with no net and you'll go likely go SPLAT!

Whether you are operating a boot camp in the park or a facility with amenities and employees, you need a business plan along with a secure foundation of capital to support you. Most new businesses fail within the first three years, and the leading cause is undercapitalization. Spend time with an accountant and your MASTERMIND team (more on this later) determining how much money you'll need at both start-up and throughout the first 24-36 months before you take the leap.

If you have been in business for a period of more than two or three years, then you already know it wasn't as easy as you anticipated. Something always comes up. Things seem to cost more than they should. The money you brought in didn't flow as fast as you thought it would. You've learned more about business, money, and the business of money during this time than any classroom could ever have taught you.

This book is a collection of my top lessons as a studio owner for the last twenty years and as a fitness professional for over a quarter of a century (sounds more impressive to say it this way).

I hope something in here reaches you.

I hope you take a required action, whether that means earning what you deserve, protecting what you have, making your money work for you or simply improving the way you think and talk about money. There is an opportunity to do both meaningful and fulfilling work in fitness, and I hope that this book helps you to find the financial fulfillment you deserve as well.

Starting to Think and Talk About Money

Let me ask you a question:

**How much money do you deserve
to make per year?**

Base your answer on your knowledge, education and certifications. Factor in your skill set, work ethic, or unique abilities. What if you include the results you deliver, the passion you have, and the countless unseen hours of thought you put into your work?

How much money do you deserve to make per year?

Be specific. There is no right or wrong number other than what you feel.

- $50K per year?
- $100K per year?
- $200K per year?
- More than one million dollars per year?

Yes, there are fitness professionals who earn more than one million dollars per year!

Now don't say $5 million per year UNLESS you are providing $5 million worth of value. This isn't pie in the sky thinking. This is self-assessment.

What is the value of your service?

How much do you deserve annually?

Write that number down either in this book or on a separate sheet of paper.

Got it?

Good.

Now, turn to the next page…

How much money did you earn last year?

**What did your W-2, 1099 or
IRS Form 1040 show?**

**When you add up all of your income
within the last year, does it equal the number
you said you deserve?**

For most, if not all of you, the numbers aren't equal, and this, my friends, is the biggest problem our industry faces – insufficient compensation relative to time and work!

Let's begin by accepting the fact that we all have a relationship with money, and like any relationship, mutual needs have to be met. If you poured yourself into a romantic relationship, or perhaps a friendship, and didn't feel that you were receiving back what you put in, what would happen? Resentment, maybe? Would you consider leaving such a relationship? This has been happening in the fitness industry for far too long, and it is like a dirty little secret. No one likes to talk about it. After all, no one got into the fitness industry to "make money." Yet many leave because of a failure to do so. Talk about irony!

We fit pros work out of love, but love doesn't pay the bills. In 2009, during the worst days of the recession, **American Express** didn't care how much I loved my clients or that I hadn't taken a paycheck in over a month. There I stood at COSTCO with a cart full of stuff, staring down at the credit card terminal that simply read DECLINED.

My story certainly isn't unique. The number one reason why people leave the fitness industry is because they need to make more money. But you can't make more money until you become more comfortable thinking and talking about it.

In the pages to follow we will discuss some simple rules of money – how to earn it, grow it, and protect it. Whether you are an instructor at a big box gym, a small studio, or a business owner yourself, I'm going to get you to think about money in a way you never have before.

*Get comfortable thinking
and talking about money
or
get comfortable not having
enough of it.*

#Frankism

I

THE FIRST RULE OF MONEY:

Don't Lose Money

No ONE INTENTIONALLY sets out to lose money. Do they?

Are you knowingly losing money in your fitness business? If so, where? What is it costing you?

I would suggest that either in this book, or on a separate sheet of paper, you begin to add up the big savings that little changes can yield.

Here are some simple suggestions to get you started on saving more of your hard-earned money.

Comparison Shop

Spend a few minutes comparing prices on the equipment you purchase from the many vendors available online (medicine balls, bands, tubing, towels, mats, t-shirts, etc.) Just a few dollars here and there added up throughout the many orders per year can easily save you a few hundred dollars. Better yet, develop relationships with particular suppliers and get ongoing discounts. Due to some of the relationships I've cultivated over the years, I receive discounts of 15-30% on all orders from some of the top suppliers and equipment manufacturers in the industry (Perform Better, LifeFitness, etc.). In fact, during the most recent facelift to my existing studio, I was able to save thousands of dollars with such techniques.

Another area to comparison shop is on your Payroll Service. Assuming you are running a real business with both payroll and the timely submission of proper taxes, I strongly encourage you to outsource this service. Here's why – in the event of a filing issue or a technical accounting flaw, the payroll service assumes the responsibility (and headache) of correcting the problem. The last thing you want to do is sit on the phone with the IRS trying to correct a tax issue from three years ago. Time is money, and like the first rule of money states – "Don't lose money!" Put this in the hands of a professional payroll service.

I used ADP Payroll for over fifteen years and never had an issue. They handled all aspects of our payroll, tax submission, direct deposits and 401(k) allocations. However, it was, according to my accountant, too expensive for a business of my size. So, I looked around and discovered GUSTO (formerly Zen Payroll). They handled the same services as ADP without issue and saved me over $1,000 per year. I have been with them for the last three years and thus far have been very happy with them.

Shop around!

Negotiate for Better Rates and Fees from Your Bank

During the slow time of year for your business, gather your current bank statements and walk into the local branch of your business bank. Better yet, call a few days in advance to schedule a meeting with a business banking officer. Tell them that you are always receiving offers from other banks and would like to know what they can do to lower your account maintenance fees, merchant fees (credit card processing costs), etc. The banking industry is a numbers game, and they will quite often drop your fees a small percent to keep you happy. This number may seem negligible, but when you consider the number of transactions annually, it can save you hundreds, or possibly thousands, of dollars a year. I suggest doing this each December or January.

Don't let the fear of having to transfer everything over to a new bank stop you. Your new bank will handle all of the messy work for you. They want your business, as a new account represents new revenue for them.

"It's not personal, Sonny. It's strictly business."

- Michael Corleone

Tackle Your Business Debt

If you have credit card debt in your business (or personally) this has to be addressed. Credit card debt is like a slow cancer to your financial health. You don't realize the damage it's causing because it's so subtle.

Here's a question:

Assuming a traditional credit card rate of 16-21%, how long will it take you to pay off a $2000 balance if you make the minimum monthly payment?

The answer is 18.5 years!!

Think about that. You pay the minimum suggested amount, and in just 18.5 years you can be free and clear of the bill for something you haven't had or used in over 17 years.

Crazy, right?

Well, not any more.

My suggestion is to always pay more than the minimum and to make payments bi-weekly rather than monthly. The interest on your balance compounds daily, so the quicker you can apply money to the principal, the faster you can pay off the balance. In simplest terms, it's better to pay $50 every two weeks than $100 per month. Check out (online) one of the debt payment calculators to see the actual savings – but trust me, it's a smarter way to handle debt.

If your credit is good, talk to your business bank about a consolidation loan. The monthly minimum will be higher but you'll eliminate the debt significantly quicker and spend less in interest over time. Again, pay more than the minimum and pay *bi-weekly* as opposed to monthly.

Remember the first rule of money: ***"Don't lose money!"***

Don't Be Penny Wise and Pound Foolish

Back in 2010 a friend of mine, "Doug," was a top trainer at a local club and competing business. He worked about thirty hours per week, and the club was charging about $80 per hour for his services at the time. Doug was approaching thirty years of age and was without health insurance. He went to his boss and inquired about receiving health insurance through the company. His boss, a small business owner, gave the socially acceptable answer of,

"Doug, we are a small business. We cannot afford it."

During a casual dinner and a few bottles of wine with me, he inquired if my company provided such a benefit to my instructors. My answer was a resounding, "YES!"

Within six months, Doug was working for me. He brought over a large number of his existing clients and was soon working thirty hours a week in my studio, where we were charging about $90 per hour for his services.

Let's do some simple math:

Doug brought in about $2400 per week at his former club – or $9,600 a month – which equals $115,200 a year.

A health insurance premium would have cost the company about $400 per month or $4,800 per year at the time.

Even if the company only paid 50% of the premium, this would have cost them $2,400 a year. Instead, by saying they couldn't afford it, it cost them $115,200 in revenue. Think about that.

Now let's look at it from this perspective. If someone was going to bring you in over $115K in revenue, would you spend $2,400 to acquire that person? Yeah, that's what I did.

I'm not encouraging you to go out and poach other trainers or coaches, but I am saying that you need to wake up to the reality of business. Great talent will always seek an environment that supports, encourages and compensates their greatness. Don't let a great trainer walk out the door with clients and dollars because you want to save a few bucks. Sadly, this happens all the time.

The truth is that providing health insurance, a 401(k), continuing education or other benefits isn't as expensive as you think, especially if you require your trainers or coaches to have some "skin in the game." This provides a benefit to them and is a cost savings investment to you and your business.

Pricing Your Services

Another silly way that too many businesses or fitness professionals lose money is by selling large packages or annual memberships – basically, any pricing structure that says *"if you agree to buy more and stay longer, I'll charge you less per session/month."*

Let's again use some simple math:

Trainer "Bob" charges $800 for ten sessions or $1,400 for twenty sessions. This means he gets $80 per session for the first option or $70 per session for the second option. This also means that with the second option, he is waiting longer for *less* money.

Wait, what?

Think about it, would you like more money sooner or less money later? Too many businesses and fitness professionals cause great harm to their cash flow due to similar pricing structures.

> *Cash flow is the lifeblood*
> *of your business!*
>
> #Frankism

Don't focus on the size of your sales. It doesn't matter what your future receivables are if you don't have the cash on hand to get you through the day.

My suggestion is to sell small packages, if you go that route. Recurring revenue is always best! For those using membership or EFT models, switch to a monthly fee and don't discount for a commitment of time. If you insist on selling an annual membership because you want to reward people for their commitment, then ask for the year's dues up front and discount the payment. That's a true commitment to the year!

The value and/or quality of your services don't diminish over time and neither should your pricing.

Insurance

This is an area you've got covered, right?

I hope so, because accidents happen and when they do, it's seldom simple.

There are three types of professional insurance that you need to pay attention to if you own a business, especially a brick and mortar facility.

1. **Liability Insurance**

I have a friend, "Mark," who owns a great training studio in Brooklyn, NY. His business was growing, and he needed to start looking for a new coach to help teach some of his classes. One of his best students, "Betty," approached him about becoming an instructor. She was recently certified and really loved his program. They both agreed to have her participate in more classes to help her improve the cues, tempo, format and skills she needed to take over the class herself one day.

During a routine exercise one night, Betty tripped and fell, breaking both of her wrists. Needless to say, having both her wrists in hard casts for 6-8 weeks was problematic for her and her ability to function in everyday life. Her husband was not too happy, either. They threatened to sue Mark, and eventually did.

Now, Mark's immediate concern was Betty's long-term prognosis (she has since recovered), but he also was now receiving nasty emails, harassing phone calls, and demands for payment of medical bills and other expenses. Fortunately, Mark had liability insurance, and he brought his insurance company in to act on his behalf. They responded to the plaintiff, Betty, and this saved Mark the time and inconvenience of having to deal with this during the discovery, investigation, and ultimate resolution of the matter. In the end, there was no negligence on Mark's part, but without a proper team of professionals to work through the facts and protect Mark's interests, this could have been costly in both time and money.

2. **Property Insurance**

If you own a studio, you'll also need property insurance. This will protect you when things beyond your control affect your operation.

Take my friend, Jarod, who owned a great club in Beaverton, Oregon. A few years back, he was getting ready to teach a class in the main room. In this room, there was floor-to-ceiling glass facing the parking lot. At the same time, a young woman was pulling into a parking space in front of the building. Apparently distracted by her phone, she stepped on the gas rather than the brake, and within seconds, she smashed right into the building. The front end of her car stopped just feet away from people warming up in class. Fortunately, no one was injured.

Clearly, she was responsible. Obviously, her insurance company would pay for the damage. But do you think her insurance company thought, *"Hey, let's spring into action and get this fixed right away, because Jarod has classes to teach?"*

No. Just like any insurance company that has to spend money, they wanted to conduct interviews, gather the facts, make a determination with regard to who had been culpable, and what, in their opinion, the true damages were. That was going to take a while…

Fortunately, Jarod had property insurance. With one phone call, they sprang into action. They had the window boarded up almost immediately. They replaced the window, and their team protected Jarod's interests by going after the young woman's insurance company.

Once again, the time and money saved cannot be measured.

3. **Business Interruption Insurance**

There are two types of people who know about this kind of insurance; those who wish they had it, and those who are glad they do. Many business owners, when pricing a comprehensive insurance policy for a club or studio, might be tempted to save some money and forgo this type of insurance. Don't!

The only time you'll need this insurance is when the business is shut down and revenues aren't coming in. The last thing you want to worry about during a time like this is, "How am I going to fund my obligations?"

Sure, given the circumstances, you might not have to pay the rent, or possibly other expenses, but any loans, taxes, utilities, insurance premiums, credit card payments, or other fees will still come due. Depending on how long you are shut down, how long could the business pay its obligations without a supply of revenue? For most fitness businesses, the answer is not long at all.

In 2006, I received a phone call on a Saturday that "some water was coming from the laundry room at work." I assumed that the washing machine sprung a leak, and I instructed my team to shut the washing machine off and place some towels down to absorb the water. A short while later another call came in.

"There is dirty water backing up in the showers and coming out of the locker room!"

Like Batman racing to the scene, I hopped in my car – it was Saturday morning, so my Superhero suit was a baggy sweatsuit and a backwards ball-cap – and arrived at the studio to see water coming from every imaginable corner of the building. WTF? I wasn't sure who to call first. Carpet cleaners? A plumber? My priest? Water was everywhere.

The plumber was the first to arrive, and I knew it wasn't good when he said, *"I've never seen anything like this!"*

After some inspecting of the building and the unpleasant scent now beyond compare, he determined that there was a city sewer backup occurring. An immediate call was placed to our Township's Department of Public Works (DPW). You can imagine how easy it was to get a *live person* on the phone on a Saturday night. By the time the DPW arrived, it was Monday morning. The water had stopped rising, and much of it had been pumped out, but the damage was done. Every inch of flooring throughout the building needed to be ripped up. All of the insulation, sheetrock, and carpets needed to be replaced. While my landlord picked up the cost of the damage repair, and was obviously not going to hold me responsible for the rent, who would pay the health insurance premium that month, the loan obligation I had on the business, and what about the equipment lease?

Fortunately, I had a small amount of business interruption insurance. This covered my expenses during the six weeks that we were shut down. My trainers and coaches received "temporary unemployment insurance," which they had as employees, not independent contractors, and I took a weeklong vacation while the studio underwent construction. When we re-opened, the place looked, felt and smelled great. There was new energy and an appreciation for having come through the adversity. But for me, and hopefully you, there was a valuable lesson learned.

*Insurance is something you pay
for that you never want to use
but are glad to have when you do.*

Plan the Divorce Before the Marriage

When relationships end, it's usually a difficult time to agree upon terms. Someone always feels slighted. Someone is usually angry. Worse yet, someone may be a relative. It's always best to negotiate who gets what in the beginning in order to simplify the terms at the end. In the beginning of a business partnership – and most relationships, generally – everyone is optimistic and agreeable. What better time to have friendly discussions with your lawyers about the things that are *unlikely* to occur?

In 2008, I decided to relocate my studio a few miles away. We had outgrown our existing spot, and I was incredibly optimistic about my business, my team, the economy, my health – I mean, what could possibly go wrong?

I found an available 4,500 sq. ft. office suite in a class "A" building and signed on to a ten-year lease. Rather than have the landlord build out the studio and factor the cost into my rent, I made the long-term decision to negotiate a less expensive lease and construct the studio at my own cost. To finance the construction, I applied for and received a $300k SBA (Small Business Association) loan. I had a recently constructed home as collateral, money in the bank, and excellent credit. They gladly handed me the money, and I eagerly accepted it.

Something I noticed at the time was that my younger brother, who had become an excellent trainer, was often viewed as "Frank's brother," rather than as a man in his own right. No one wants to feel that they have their job because their older brother owns the place. While not the perfect older brother, I've always wanted to protect him. So, I came up with an idea. I would offer him the opportunity to buy 1/3 of the business, giving him a piece of ownership in our business. I figured with $300k of debt, and a ten-year lease now resting in my name, I would sell him 1/3 of the business for $100k and together we would grow the business, make joint decisions, and pay off our obligations. Not technically the most detailed of plans, but most small businesses are financed through exactly this kind of hopeful enthusiasm.

In late 2008, he secured a loan of $100k from our father, and we were now partners. No sooner had we opened the new studio when the economy tanked, the recession hit, and we were starving for cash to meet our obligations. Over the next several years, we were on unstable footing. There was staff turnover, paychecks were reduced, and there were weeks at a time where I didn't even take a paycheck. Unlike before our partnership where we agreed on almost everything, we now found ourselves with different views on everything from equipment placement to staffing to the color of our t-shirts.

By 2013, things had started to turn the corner financially. We were making enough money to take regular paychecks, and our team was somewhat stable. One thing that was very apparent at this point, however, was that my brother and I now had a co-existing relationship rather than a partnership. Whether this was due to family stress outside of the workplace or professional disagreements, the fact was that we were now tolerating each other rather than working together.

In early 2014, I began having some issues with my voice. At first, I was told it was just a cold, then a sinus infection, likely laryngitis, possibly acid reflux, maybe idiopathic vocal cord paralysis. Several months later, it was determined that I had thyroid cancer, which would require surgery. While trying to wrap my mind around what was to come, my brother came to me with some news of his own – he was moving to North Dakota.

What? North Dakota?

I didn't think people really lived there, let alone *move* there?!

He explained that he had met a girl, and she received a job offer there. He wanted to go with her. I was happy for him. At the same time, I was happy for me, because I knew that the unspoken stress of our disconnection wasn't good for the business. So, I hugged him and told him that I was proud of him for making such a bold move.

He asked what would happen to his shares in the business. I told him to give me a few days to figure something out, and we would discuss how we would handle this. I spent the next few days scheduling surgical interviews, training clients, and trying to determine a buy-out price for his share of the business. How do you determine such a value? Small businesses often possess no actual value other than the services provided. If one person leaves an organization, what value are they contributing? I had spreadsheets, P&L statements, and tax returns examined and assessed. The glaring fact was that there was no business value to pay out. Worse yet, there was still significant business debt and obligations (in my name) to be dealt with and a business to operate. To complicate matters even more, there was the simple fact that since the beginning of our partnership, he had been paid more income than me. This was not going to be easy.

I offered him $50k in cash, although I was unsure exactly where I was going to get this. My offer took into consideration that we were halfway through the ten-year lease and the SBA loan obligation. Naturally, he wanted his entire $100k back, but that wasn't financially possible. Besides, it was *his* choice to leave, why should his financial obligation be settled and I be left with more debt than I'm comfortable with? He left disappointed, and soon thereafter our lawyers started a series of back and forth letters.

He was now in North Dakota, and I was preparing for my upcoming surgery. His lawyers wanted $125k for his shares.

We said, "No."

They requested $150k for his shares.

We said, "No."

The thing that everyone forgets in the emotion of most transactions is that something is only worth what one party is willing to pay, and what the other party is willing to part with. I wasn't willing to pay what I didn't have, and he was unwilling to accept less than what he felt he was owed. About a year after departing and rejecting my initial offer of $50k, we both spoke on the phone and agreed to settle for $20k.

There are many lessons here, depending on how you choose to look at things. If possible, try to avoid partnerships. Eventually a partner may leave, and what will happen then? Negotiate this in advance.

If you do choose to partner, don't do it out of financial convenience or emotional reasoning. Partner with someone who brings a necessary skill set and a complementary vision.

I look back and know that my heart was in the right place. Though I may have saved $30k settling with my brother, the truth is that it cost me much more than that. He and I have hardly spoken in years and this matter only further divided an already fractured relationship with my family.

> *Don't go into business with anyone, family or otherwise, unless you have clearly defined roles and terms upon how to handle the eventual ending of the partnership.*
>
> #Frankism

Avoid Taking on Debt

There will come a time when an unexpected expenditure comes along. Whenever possible, use available cash on hand to pay for such things. Unless you intend to pay with a credit card and pay off the balance at month's end, it's a slippery slope to fall down. I would suggest that all businesses maintain a minimum of one months' worth of fixed expenses (rent, loan obligations, utilities, insurance) in an emergency fund. Not being able to handle issues quickly or overpaying for essential repairs can prove quite costly in the long run.

Can you reduce your paycheck for a period of time to build up an emergency fund?

Can you ask your team to reduce their pay for an equal period of time?

Can you negotiate a period of reduced rent with your landlord during this time?

If necessary, stop making payments on a maxed-out credit card (it's worthless anyway) and funnel some of that money into your emergency fund. You'll build that surprisingly quickly with an "all-in" approach.

Don't be afraid to make the difficult choices or avoid the uncomfortable conversations when it comes to money.

> *You can't save your way to prosperity, you've got to make more money!*
>
> #Frankism

Action Steps

_____

_____

_____

_____

_____

_____

_____

_____

_____

_____

_____

_____

_____

_____

_____

_____

II

THE SECOND RULE
OF MONEY:

Make More Money

BEFORE WE START talking about how to make money in your fitness business, we need to ask ourselves, "How much money is possible? Is there a limit?"

I would argue that you are limited only by your imagination.

"Don't get so caught looking at the ceiling that you miss the sky."
-Unknown

Fitness professionals are notoriously bad at thinking about and negotiating money. It's just not what we do. It's never been a cornerstone of our industry, unlike accounting or finance, where every day is an endless conversation around numbers and dollars. Let me put this into perspective for you.

My best friend, "Jennifer," is an accountant. Specifically, she works for a firm that specializes in keeping the books for several hedge funds and high value investment trusts. Her firm charges their clients $1,600 an hour for her services.

Let me repeat that.

Her firm charges their clients *$1,600 per hour* for her services.

But here's the best part – the clients gladly pay that fee! They feel at that rate they are receiving value.

So now you know that in the world of high-end-accounting, people will charge and pay $1,600 an hour, while in the fitness industry, gym owners are afraid to raise their prices $5/month because they're afraid of losing customers. Does that seem reasonable? Do you see the disparity?

Jennifer isn't *Rain Man* doing this math in her head. She's plugging numbers into a computer and sharing the results with her clients. Meanwhile, fitness professionals are waking up at 4 a.m. to build fitness, nutrition and lifestyle routines for clients, which help to prevent heart disease, cancer, diabetes, hypertension, depression, and obesity.

And what does the average high-end personal trainer charge for such a life-changing service?

As of this writing, around $95 an hour.

Why such a disparity?

If for no other reason, it's because we don't believe there is as much perceived value for our services. We feel that there is too much competition, and we want to be careful not to price ourselves out of the market.

That's fear talking. Starbucks doesn't worry about their coffee being more expensive, and last I checked, you could get a cup of coffee anywhere. Heck, go get your hair cut or styled and you can get a cup for free!

The amount of money you can charge and earn is proportional to what you are comfortable asking for, and what you believe is possible. Know that possibilities are only limited by what you can imagine. Imagine greater financial possibilities and you'll become more comfortable asking for what you're worth.

> *"If you know what you're worth,*
> *then get what you're worth."*
> - Rocky Balboa

How to Earn More

There are only 3 ways to make money in a fitness business:

1. Charge more for what you do

This concept is simple enough, and by now you realize that you aren't earning what you deserve or what you're worth. So, what is the value of your service or membership? Write down what you truly believe you should be charging given the value you or your service provides. What is the number that you can charge that you can justify to your clients? Make a commitment to raise your fees, rates or prices to this amount. The truth is, it should be easy because the true value is probably a little higher. But this is the number that you are *comfortable* with – the number that won't get too many complaints or questions from those clients that you care about more than you care about your own needs. If there is one takeaway from this book it might be this – **charge what you are worth.**

I would suggest a fee or rate increase annually. The cost of doing business goes up every year and your prices should reflect this. It doesn't matter if it is $2 an hour or $5 a month, get comfortable raising prices each year and don't make a big production about why. Remind your clients or customers that due to an increase in business costs, there will be a slight increase in fees, effective (future date). Give them the opportunity to pre-buy if their renewal comes after (future date). Commit to continuing to provide the *highest quality service* and express your appreciation for the opportunity to serve them. A final point to remember is this: You can't be the cheapest and the best. Commit to being the best and charge appropriately.

> **Businesses that start cutting fees to attract customers enter the race to see who'll go broke first.**
>
> #Frankism

2. Get more clients or customers

This is where most business owners spend most of their time. Asking the question, how can we get more clients or customers?

Let's keep it simple.

What is working best for you regarding new client or customer acquisition?

Where do most of your clients and customers come from?

How can you do an even better job or spend more time and resources in this area?

You just told me it's working, so do more of it!

What always amazes me is when I talk with fit pros and they tell me, *"Word of mouth is my best advertising, but I want to learn about Facebook ads, or create a new LBO (low barrier offer) to attract clients who know nothing about me or have never heard of us."*

What?

That's like a golfer saying *"I often hit a hole in one with this club, but I'm thinking about switching to a different club."* Stick to what is working!

Now, if you are having success with Facebook or Instagram ads, YouTube, direct mail, flyers on windshields or anything else, pour more money into that! Anything that helps you increase the number of clients or customers is worth investing money in, and like any investment, you want the best ROI (return on investment) possible. Know that nothing will work forever except the time-tested formula of turning clients and customers into raving fans.

If you aren't sure where to begin or lack the funds (as I did) to invest in traditional marketing or advertising programs, try my 5x5 Referral Improvement Program. It's low-cost and will yield almost immediate benefits to both you and your business.

This 5x5 system has been a staple in my business for many years.

5x5 Referral System

1. **Converse with 5 clients or customers each day:** Find out what's new, how things are going, how are they feeling?

2. **Text 5 clients or customers weekly:** Just a quick message to let them know you're thinking of them.

3. **Call 5 clients or customers monthly:** Ask if there is anything you can do to make their experience with you or your business more enjoyable.

4. **Take 5 of your VIP clients or customers (those that refer others) out to dinner annually:** Bring spouses or significant others. If you're on a budget, opt for lunch or coffee.

5. **Invest a minimum of 5 days per year away from your business:** Attend conferences or workshops, continue to learn, stay inspired. When you are at your best, people take notice.

3. **Get your clients or customers to buy more from you**

What additional services can you provide that would benefit your clients or customers? Do you have a client who would clearly benefit from more training with you? If so, sit down and share with them why this would be of greater benefit to them as it relates to their wants or needs. Perhaps they train more often, or purchase other services you can provide? Example: you have a client who trains two times per week; get them to train three times per week.

Your clients and customers want the best outcome. If something you offer would improve their outcome, why not address this? Ideas might include: specialized workshops, one on one coaching, apparel, massage or bodywork services.

Maybe it's simply greater access to the gym facility. One of my friends, "Matt" made a small investment into setting up a 24-hour gym access system for his personal training studio, and now pays his entire monthly overhead from just this membership revenue. What additional options have you considered?

If there is one suggestion I would make to all fitness professionals, it would be to align yourself with a nutrition program and integrate it fully into your fitness business, whether that be nutrition coaching or a nutrition line.

If you aren't addressing nutrition with your clients, you are ignoring the reality of your clients' or customers' lifestyle.

The problem for most of your clients or customers isn't their workout or training, it's what they are putting into their bodies. Fitness professionals are great at talking about how "you can't out-exercise a bad diet." Yet, all they seem to focus on or feel comfortable charging money for, is access to or the instruction of, an apparently ineffective exercise program. Why not sell what works?

I'm not here to sell a particular product or program of nutrition. There are many excellent ones, and I would suggest you find one that aligns with your philosophy and have the integrity to use the program or product yourself. Personally, I drink SHAKEOLOGY daily. I absolutely love it. But that's me, and I have no problem sharing my beliefs about the product. Other friends of mine swear by PRU-VIT, which is a KETO-based nutrition line. Perhaps you want people to eat only a whole-food-based diet. Great. Look into Precision Nutrition coaching for your business. The point is that nutrition is a critical piece of a fitness program, and as fitness professionals, it is our job to provide complete solutions and deliver results. Improve your client or customer results, and you'll also improve your top line (revenue) growth.

Action Steps

_____

_____

_____

_____

_____

_____

_____

_____

_____

_____

_____

_____

_____

_____

_____

_____

III

THE THIRD RULE
OF MONEY:

*Protect and Grow
Your Wealth*

SO, YOU'VE GOTTEN this far.

Congratulations!

Actually, that line was for me. You see, when I started writing this book, I didn't think I'd get past the first paragraph, so I'm a little surprised to find myself here.

Now maybe you have flipped through the pages to get to what could be considered "the good stuff" but then, of course, you'd have missed the first rule of money, and a few simple tips on how to grow your fitness business revenues more simply and sanely.

This section deals with a problem that I want more fitness professionals to have to deal with:

"What do I do once I start to actually make money from my business?"

There are several approaches one can take when it comes to handling your finances.

- For a fee, you can hire a money manager who will allocate a certain amount of money to you for basic expenses, and this person will invest, pay bills, submit payments, collect earnings, and cover all aspects of your financial life. Professional athletes, lottery winners or those who achieve sudden riches would be well-served to invest in such a service.

- Take 20% of your earnings, place that into a conservative savings or investment plan, and then go spend the rest on whatever is left over. Perhaps this is not the most detailed strategy, but in 20-30 years, you should be able to enjoy a comfortable retirement, and along the way you'll have funds available for emergencies. This also allows you the freedom to spend however you choose based on the budgetary discretion remaining.

- A more practical approach for most fitness professionals is to begin educating yourself on some wealth building and wealth protecting fundamentals. Building a team that includes an attorney, accountant, investment professional, insurance agent, and an advisory board that understands you and your business is essential for success. Do you have such a team?

Earlier we spoke about the need to have proper insurance to protect your fitness business. But do you have proper insurance to protect your personal income?

Disability Insurance

Most, if not all, fitness businesses are labor intensive. You work, you get paid. You don't work, you don't get paid. Simple, right?

What happens when something prevents you from working when you want to? What happens when an injury occurs that prevents you from performing your job? How will you pay your bills?

Now you may be thinking, *"Nothing will keep me from work!"* I assure you, you're wrong.

A few years ago, I was out cycling with my friend, Liz, when we both hit a slick spot in the road and went down. I got up with some scrapes and blood. She didn't get up as quickly. She had noticeably less blood, but a noticeably broken elbow. The elbow required surgery, and she had to wear a hard cast for almost 8 weeks while the joint healed. Fortunately, the elbow was on her left side, and she was able to drive herself to and from work during this time. But what if it was her right elbow? She wouldn't be able to operate her vehicle. Remember "Betty" from earlier? She's the client who fell and broke both of her wrists. What if she was a coach or instructor or a business owner, for that matter? Could she perform her job effectively? Could you?

One of the many advantages of being an employee versus an IC (independent contractor) is that employee payroll withholdings contain a premium payment for a disability insurance program. That's right. It's not just your taxes that are taking a bite out of your paycheck. You also have disability insurance in the event of an accident or illness that prevents you from working. Considering how a wipe out can wipe you out, I'd say it's money well spent. If you are an IC and are training in various facilities or running boot camps somewhere, I would strongly urge you to look into a disability insurance program to protect yourself in the event of such an occurrence. A great place to start would be with your professional insurance agent or perhaps a company like AFLAC. You just made that 'quack' sound, didn't you?

Auto Insurance

This is not a topic often discussed at any of the professional industry trade shows, but it should be. As a business owner, you possess an investment or asset. If you are found to be at fault in an auto-accident, that could jeopardize that asset and other assets you own. Now you may be thinking, *"But I've got insurance!"*

My question is, "But do you have adequate coverage?"

Here are some simple questions to help you answer that:

What is the (BIL) "Bodily Injury Liability Coverage" on your policy? Do you have the state minimum value?

What is the (PIP) "Personal Injury Protection" coverage limit? Do you have any idea what I'm talking about? Don't worry, most people have no clue. This means you're in good company, potentially with inadequate insurance.

That little green gecko that likes to save you money on car insurance just might be doing so by giving you the minimum requirements. You may have lower premiums but an increased exposure to costs and damages that exceed your coverage.

> *When deciding how much coverage you need, make sure you're covered for an amount equal to the total value of your assets.*
>
> #Frankism

Auto insurance is a collection of different policies that cover you in different ways. Here's how they break down:

- **Liability coverage** – These policies help cover liability and expenses when you're at fault in an accident. The money will go to the people you hit, but it won't cover the people in your car.

- **Bodily Injury Liability (BIL)** – This policy pays for the medical expenses of people injured in a crash in which you're at fault. You'll often see BIL policies described as a "20/50" policy or a "100/300" policy. These numbers describe the maximum dollar amount the policy will pay for a single person's injuries and the maximum for all the injuries sustained by all the occupants of the other car. For example, a 20/50 policy will pay a maximum of $20,000 for a single person's injuries, and up to $50,000 total for the injuries of everyone in the car you hit.

- **Property Damage Liability** – This policy pays for damage done to the other car if you're at fault in an accident. Property liability is sometimes referred to alongside BIL as a third number, so a 20/50/10 liability package will cover up to $10,000 for damages to the other car.

The following policies cover you and your car in an accident:

- **Personal Injury Protection (PIP)** – This covers you and your passengers' medical expenses after an accident. If you lose time at work because of your injuries, this policy may also cover lost wages.

- **Collision** – This policy covers repairs to your car after an accident.

Nearly every state requires car owners to carry auto insurance, and most states have required minimum values for different policies. If you don't carry insurance, the state can impound your vehicle. Find out your state's minimums. The minimum coverage isn't necessarily all you should have. New Jersey, for example, requires car owners to carry a 15/30/5 liability package. If you're involved in a serious accident, it's possible that an individual's medical expenses could exceed $15,000, or a group's expenses could total more than $30,000. In addition, $5,000 for car repairs isn't a lot, considering that the average car now costs a little more than $20,000.

The reason this is important is because you're on the hook when costs exceed your coverage limits. That's why many people opt for policies that cover more than required minimums, particularly if they have assets that can be seized to pay for repairs and medical care.

Speak to your insurance agent to make sure that your exposure is minimized and you have the coverage you need!

Life Insurance

You won't need this type of insurance coverage if you don't plan on dying. However, if you plan on participating in the afterlife, then this might be something to consider. Maybe?

I bought my first life insurance plan when I was twenty-eight years old. I had no wife, no kids, and no thoughts of dying anytime soon (or as of this writing) – but I did have thoughts of paying my father back, who had just loaned me money to open my business. Of course, I was going to pay him back, but what if, God forbid, something happened to me? In the event of my early demise, how would my father recoup his loan? A simple term life policy protected him and was the responsible thing for me to do to ensure that he wouldn't lose both his son and his money.

Do you have loans to investors? Do you have a spouse who will be responsible for a mortgage? Do you have children you want to provide for? Who will provide for them in the event of your untimely passing? Consider life insurance as peace of mind during the most trying of times.

There are actually several types of life insurance, but I'll discuss the two most common that you should know about:

Term Life – Insurance that you basically "rent" for a period or term. This allows you to enjoy steady premiums for a number of years and with a pre-determined payout amount to the beneficiary.

Whole Life – Insurance that you "own" and grows in cash value in addition to providing a payout amount. The premiums will generally be higher than a term life policy.

Many factors will determine which, if any, life insurance policy is appropriate for you. Speak with a qualified agent to discuss your options or needs.

Medical/Health Insurance

When I started writing this book, it was mandatory in the United States for all people to purchase medical/health insurance. As of today, the mandate has been stripped away. In my opinion, this is NOT a good thing. Sooner or later, you're going to need this type of insurance and when you do, you can't afford to be without it.

Do you know what the leading cause of personal bankruptcy is in the US? <u>The inability to pay ones' medical or hospital costs.</u> Don't believe that it is only the uninsured who are at risk. Similar to your auto policy, you may have insurance, but do you have proper coverage?

Rare or serious diseases or injuries can easily result in hundreds of thousands of dollars in medical bills – bills that can quickly wipe out savings and retirement accounts, college education funds or home equity. Once these have been exhausted, bankruptcy may be the only option.

But I'm healthy...
nothing is going to happen to me!

In 2014, a raspy voice that was initially believed to be a cold or sinus infection was, months later, revealed by ultrasound and confirmed though a biopsy, to be thyroid cancer. On July 2nd of that year I underwent a six-hour thyroidectomy (complete removal), along with the removal of several cancerous lymph nodes in my neck, and the surgical excision of a tumor on my right vocal cord. I spent one night in the hospital and left the following afternoon. Over the next eighteen months, I underwent several more ultrasounds, biopsies, various scans, blood work and three days of "RAI" (Radioactive Iodine) therapy in isolation. The total cost billed to my insurance company from start to finish was $180,000. Thankfully, when all my total out-of-pocket expenses were calculated, the cost to me was under $3,000. In addition, I'll take Synthroid daily for the rest of my life, which would add about $200 a month for life in prescriptive costs without insurance.

What if it happened to you? Do you have the $3,000 for deductibles and copays? Imagine not having insurance at all. Do you have the $180,000? If not, don't worry. You will still find a public hospital to take excellent care of you, and you can pay them the $180,000 over time through their financing department. How long do you think this will take you to pay back (and yes, they'll charge you interest)? The correct answer is usually NEVER! You'll pay medical bills for the rest of your life, unless you tap into your other assets or savings. Once those resources are gone, you're on the hook for the balance.

The ACA (Affordable Care Act) or its nickname, "Obamacare," required insurance companies to remove both the annual and lifetime caps on coverage benefits and the denial of pre-existing conditions. This raised premiums as more coverage was included in modern policies. In my opinion, it beats having a cheap policy that doesn't cover the treatment, procedure or therapy when you need it the most.

If you have coverage, make sure you understand it. If you don't have medical/health insurance, I would suggest you rethink your reasoning.

Growing Your Wealth

Earlier we learned how providing health insurance to your employees wasn't just a smart move to protect losing great people, but an effective tool at possibly recruiting great people, too. Offering benefits to potential fitness professionals is a smart investment.

Another smart investment for all fitness professionals is to participate in a qualified retirement plan. There are four basic plans that I will cover:

401(k) – These plans are administered through your company and allow you to invest pre-tax dollars into an investment portfolio of your choosing. Most portfolios contain mutual funds of either stocks, bonds or a combination of both. All monies paid into your account grow tax-deferred until the time of your withdrawal. Any monies contributed (not required) by your company also go into your account tax-free until the time of your withdrawal. There is a maximum contribution of $18,500 annually as of this writing, but that amount increases every year. Also note, there are age limit withdrawals and penalties for early withdrawal of these funds. There are also certain exceptions to this. 401(k) plans are commonly used today and are a great incentive to encourage savings and wealth building for yourself or your employees.

Simple IRA – Similar to a 401(k) – think of it as a 401(k) for small business. It allows you to invest pre-tax dollars into an investment portfolio with a maximum contribution of up to $12,500 or $15,500 (if over 50 years of age) annually, but unlike a 401(k), this plan requires the company to make a contribution annually. The amount of that contribution varies by what the company chooses during the set-up, and this may be modified at a later date.

Both of these plans can be administered for your business through a professional payroll company. Fidelity and Vanguard are two of the largest mutual fund families handling these types of plans.

For those not owning or working for a company that provides or qualifies for such plans, there are Roth and traditional IRAs.

Roth IRA – A retirement plan that you set up individually and fund with post-tax dollars. Money will be withdrawn from your checking or savings account and deposited in a portfolio of your choosing. The current maximum contribution allotment is $5,500 or $6,500 (if over 50 years of age) annually. There are income limits on those who are eligible to qualify for such a plan. All monies at time of eligible withdrawal are tax-free.

Traditional IRA – Unlike the Roth IRA, this plan offers you the ability to deduct your contribution from your current taxes. However, all monies at time of withdrawal are subject to taxation.

Yes, you can contribute to a company-sponsored plan and an IRA, but there are income limits that may affect your options. These are subject to change, so learn more at **www.irs.gov/retirement-plans.**

One suggestion I will offer for those choosing to go-it-alone, is to consider using VANGUARD as your portfolio fund company. You can't control the rate of return percentage of your investments, but you can control the costs. VANGUARD has the lowest costs in the industry, period. Even when it comes to growing your money, the first rule of money applies. "Don't lose money!"

Despite the above suggestion, it is important to understand that the lowest cost doesn't always equal the best decision. The best choice is usually to work with a CFP (Certified Financial Planner) to discuss your risk, options and the proper allocations for you.

The Best Investment

Over time, there is one investment that will have the greatest impact on your financial well-being. Investing in this area will offer you an ROI (Return On Investment) of 3,000%. There is no stock, index or (speculative) internet currency that can provide you with this kind of return. In fact, if you aren't investing money in this area, you aren't growing financially, personally or professionally to your fullest potential.

What is this investment?

Your own Personal Development.

Nothing else offers its potential for growth. So how does one begin to invest in their personal development?

Fitness: A good place to start for most people, including fitness professionals, is in the area of personal fitness, and here's why – nothing will have a more noticeable impact to your external appearance than good health. Sickness, sedentary living, poor dietary habits or addictions all take their toll on one's quality of life, performance and influence. Simply put, if you expect to make a living touting the benefits of a fitness lifestyle, you should be a product of your product, for the good of your business as well as your own quality of life.

Books: Another great opportunity for personal development is reading books. Where else can you nourish your mind with the wisdom of others for under $39? But the key to reading books isn't to read as many as you can; the way you get the most value from any book is to read it several times. Go deeper. As you grow in life, different chapters will speak to you at different times, much like this book. Today you might not be thinking about health insurance for employees as you could be a *solopreneur,* but a year from now, you might have an employee to think about. Books offer you a chance to revisit them and extract what you need, when you need it. A fine investment indeed!

Workshops and Conferences: Live events are opportunities for growth because they expose you to new ideas. Similar to books, you can extract great value by attending workshops or conferences annually, even if the material hasn't changed, as hopefully you have. Experience is a wonderful thing; it forms us and helps us to develop opinions. So when a new you meets relevant information, your perspective and clarity on the subject matter becomes much more valuable. Even a single takeaway can make a difference as you serve others and grow yourself.

Retreats: Getting away is a valuable investment as you are the engine that drives your fitness business, and no matter how powerful or ambitious that engine, you can't utilize your full potential with a dead battery. It is essential to get away and turn off the noise so that you can be fully charged when it's time to turn it on. Don't seek a retreat that simply adds more sleep to your schedule, although sleep is a great thing. Seek ones that challenge you somehow. I have several friends who have spent days at a monastery (no phone, TV, talking or noise of any kind) with just their inner thoughts. Talk about turning off the noise! Of course, this might be a little extreme for most, but at any type of retreat, you will hopefully have some sort of breakdown which allows you to have the needed breakthrough. At such moments, there is great power.

Mastermind Groups: If you want to improve at anything in life, you can likely do it alone. But to make real progress, attain success or become truly the best version of yourself personally or professionally, you need a team.

Who's on your team?

Think for a moment.

When you are contemplating a business decision, who do you consult? Who do you share knowledge with when you discover a better way? Who keeps you accountable to do what you said you would do? Who lets you know that the work you are doing isn't aligned with the goals you have stated? Are you trying to cross the ocean alone or do you have others at your side who share an equal ambition to make it to the other side?

A MASTERMIND group isn't a program where you show up with problems and get helpful solutions. A MASTERMIND group is a collection of individuals working together so that everyone can succeed. Like most things in life, you'll get out of it what you put into it. Personally speaking, joining the Todd Durkin Mastermind Program in 2009 was perhaps the greatest investment I ever made. Although I wasn't sure how I could afford it at the time, I knew the potential cost of continuing alone was more than I could bear.

Since that time, not only has my business grown year after year, I became a better leader and a stronger person. Today I coach my own team in the Todd Durkin Mastermind, and I help others navigate their path by helping them to develop the clarity needed and the accountability required. Most fitness professionals have an *"I'll do this on my own"* mentality. I, too, thought this way for a long time. Looking at it now, I can tell you that investing your time and money into building up a team around you isn't just essential for growing your revenues, profits and wealth, it's the best way to grow as a person.

Action Steps

_____

_____

_____

_____

_____

_____

_____

_____

_____

_____

_____

_____

_____

_____

_____

IV

Develop Your Game Plan

No TWO FITNESS businesses are ever exactly alike. Where they are similar, however, is in their basic need for proper insurance. Every fitness business needs to be prepared for the unexpected. They need clearly-defined contracts to determine who gets what when the unlikely-to-occur actually happens, and they need to encourage top line (revenue) growth.

Remember what we have discussed:

Do you possess the proper insurance and maintain adequate insurance as discussed earlier?

Do you have (if applicable) partnership agreements? Including what happens in the event of the death or passing of one of the partners?

How will you grow your business?

Are you charging appropriately? You can't be the cheapest and still be the best, which path will you choose?

Do you have a system in place to encourage referrals or acquire new leads from outside sources?

For the record, I believe so strongly in encouraging growth through referrals because when times were tough, I had no money for marketing or advertising. Today I spend less than five percent of our revenues on marketing materials and promotions. That amount works for me and my business. What you spend isn't important, it's the ROI that matters most. Do what works! Don't be afraid to give up what doesn't. Never forget that nothing works better for lead generation than delivering a great experience and consistent results. For the last 20-plus years this philosophy has yielded the best results as I seek to drive revenues.

At the end of the day, the role of your fitness business, or any business, really, is to make YOU, its owner, money. What you do with your money is up to you, but as we've discussed, it's never a bad idea to prepare for when the winds of change blow you in an unwanted direction.

Invest in professional attorneys, agents, accountants and financial planners to determine the appropriate needs for your business and lifestyle.

Save some money for the future and invest a portion of your income for coaching your greatest potential asset, YOU.

That's not just a practical, smart money move, it's a priceless one.

Action Steps

_____

_____

_____

_____

_____

_____

_____

_____

_____

_____

_____

_____

_____

_____

_____

_____

_____

A FINAL LESSON...

I got by most of my life on good luck, passion and occasional grit. Not a bad plan, really, until it no longer worked. When that happened, it was time for me to learn a lesson long overdue!

Growth doesn't happen until you BUILD a foundation for it.

"Rick, I'm reading all of these books on goal-setting, developing a successful mindset, and ways to attract new clients and customers. But I've got little to show for it. In fact, I've cut my salary in half, stopped contributing to my 401(k), and feel like I'm working harder for less!"

My friend, Rick, is a simple man with a very Obi Wan Kenobi-like way about him, so if anybody was going to have the fix for what was ailing my business, I knew it would be him.

"Frank, I've got the solution. Write this down so you don't forget it."

As I reached for pen and paper, I began to anticipate what he might say: Offer a discount? Ask for referrals? Let go of an under-performing employee?

"OK Rick, I'm ready!"

"Frank, go to the Home Depot. When you're there, pick up the following items:

- *A clay pot*
- *Potting soil*
- *Plant or Flower seed"*

WHAT?

"Rick, I need personal training clients. I need to GROW my revenue. How is this going to help me?"

"You can't experience GROWTH unless you have a foundation for growth. And building a foundation for anything requires that you don't ignore the fundamentals. You don't appreciate or have the patience for the fundamentals, and until you BUILD that, you can't grow anything, Frank!"

Loud EXHALE to let him know that I didn't like where this was heading.

"Ok, then what?"

"Place the soil in the clay pot. Then add your plant seed to the soil, and cover with more soil. Add some water and leave it alone."

Confused?

"That's it?"

"No, of course not. All you've done is create the proper structure and environment for growth (Pot and Soil) and inserted a future plan (Seed). Now you've got to position it in your house so that it gets several hours of direct sunlight (Energy) and give it some water (Nourishment) every few days. Then just sit back and watch

the growth that will occur when you have the fundamentals of a proper environment, a solid plan, and you give that plan the energy and nourishment it requires."

But?!

"Rick, you know that I'm not the one with the patience to watch the grass grow."

"Yep, and if you want to improve at anything, you must exercise your weakness, Frank. You know that! That's why every day I want you to look at the soil first thing in the morning and ask the soil WHY AREN'T YOU GROWING?"

"Dude, you want me to complain about a pot of soil every day? How's that going to inspire growth?"

"You're doing that about your business every day. How's that working? Is that inspiring growth, or keeping you from doing what's necessary, establishing and respecting the fundamentals?"

TOUCHÉ.

"Okay, Rick, I'm understanding most of this. But how is talking/complaining to the soil a fundamental, exactly? How long do I speak to my soil for (at 5am, mind you)?"

"Questioning the process is natural, but developing patience in business, or life for that matter, is essential for your success. So, every day, go downstairs, question your soil. Say to your soil: **damn it, you've got the right environment, a good plan, and I'm giving you energy and nourishment. When are you going to show me something?** *Do this day-in, day-out, each morning without failure. But one day, you're going to go downstairs and something will break the soil surface, and as you continue to energize and feed your creation, it will continue to grow. But without those solid fundamentals, Frank, GROWTH will never occur."*

YES, OBI WAN.

So off to the Home Depot I went. I purchased a clay pot, potting soil, and palm tree seeds because I've always had a thing for palm trees. I followed the instructions as provided by Rick and I waited. At the same time, I had a meeting with my team at work: **"We need to get organized. We must focus** on not only who we serve, but why we do what we do. We need to be better, do better!" It wasn't easy, it was going to take some time, so I waited, and waited.

I don't remember exactly when what appeared to be a blade of grass emerged from the soil. I'm not exactly sure when we turned the financial corner at work. But since that time, my business revenues have grown year-after-year, my studio generated one million dollars in annual revenue and now I'm an author and speaker, helping fitness professionals to GROW financially.

You can do it, too!

This book is simply the seed, meant to plant an idea on how to EARN, GROW and PROTECT the money you deserve. But like any seed, it requires energy and attention to have a chance at growth.

Give yourself that chance.

If you want to continue this discussion join my "Smart Money Moves" page on FACEBOOK (www.facebook.com/smartmoneymovescoaching). I look forward to seeing you there.

As for my Palm Tree?

Still getting the energy and attention it deserves!

Additional Reading

The Automatic Millionaire
- David Bach

The Entrepreneur Roller Coaster
- Darren Hardy

Money: Master the Game
- Tony Robbins

The Six-Day Financial Makeover
- Robert Pagliarini

Zombie Loyalists
- Peter Shankman

Delivering Happiness
- Tony Hsieh